Power Up!
KICKING YOUR FAITH TO A NEW LEVEL
Student Journal

CONTENTS

Written by Randy Petersen, Jim Hancock, and Mitch Vander Vorst

Editor: Mitch Vander Vorst
Cover Illustration: Thomason Design Center
Cover & Text Design: Blum Graphic Design

Copyright © 1997 by *Mainstay Church Resources*
Published by Mainstay Church Resources

Unless otherwise indicated, all Scripture quotations are taken from the *Holy Bible,* New Living Translation, copyright © 1996. Used by permission of Tyndale House Publishers, Inc., Wheaton, Illinois 60189. All rights reserved.

Scripture quotations marked (NIV) are taken from the HOLY BIBLE, NEW INTER-NATIONAL VERSION®. NIV®. Copyright © 1973, 1978, 1984 by International Bible Society. Used by permission of Zondervan Publishing House. All rights reserved.

Mainstay Church Resources is the new publishing outreach of The Chapel of the Air Ministries. Our goal is to facilitate revival among God's people by helping them develop healthy spiritual habits in nine areas that always characterize genuine times of awakening. To support this goal, Mainstay Church Resources provides print and media materials including the annual 50-Day Spiritual Adventure, the Seasonal Advent Celebration, and the 4-Week Festival of Worship.

Printed in the United States of America

ISBN 1-57849-040-5

IntRoDUCtion

IT WAS MY BEST game ever. I (Randy) sat in front of the screen, my hand gripping the controller, my thumb on the fire button, shooting the mutants whenever they appeared from around a corner. I made it through four levels, facing more insane opponents each time, and I still hadn't lost a man. I was in the zone, already calculating the millions of points I was racking up, surely an all-time high. I would proudly place my initials atop the list of cyber-jockeys who'd never come close to my score.

With a blip and a fading dot, the screen went blank.

In my excitement, I had accidentally kicked the plug out of the socket. With the loss of power the game reset. It was lost. My all-time score would never be on the list.

The trauma deeply scarred me. My video-game playing was never quite the same again. Alas, I had to turn to other pursuits, like writing.

Power is important. Computers or cross-country skiing, bass guitars or baby-sitting, you need the juice to make it work. You run out of power and you're toast.

Ever try to run Windows on a 286? It takes about a decade to even get a menu.

Ever try to take an exam on no sleep? All those facts you just crammed into your noggin are just out of reach.

Ever try to shoot hoops when you haven't munched a thing in three days? Your opponent suddenly seems to have the moves of Penny Hardaway, leaving you in the dust.

Ever try to start a car with a dead battery? Click. Click. Click. Nothing. No juice.

Problem is, we often try to do the Christianity thing without any juice. This is crazy, when you think about it, because God's middle name is Power, and he offers to energize us whenever we need it. We just don't tap into the power like we should.

We go days without prayer, and then we wonder why God seems far away. We leave the Bible on the shelf collecting dust and complain that we don't have any direction in our lives. We walk on the edge of temptation and wonder why we keep falling in.

What's the answer? It's as simple as the "on" button on your TV or hair dryer. Turn on your faith! Over the next 50 days, we invite you to take some life-changing steps to tap into the intense power that's available to you. Let God power you up, kicking you to a whole new level of faith.

How to use this journal

● **Pray** that God will kick you into high gear in the next 50 days. Ask him what PowerPoints *he'd* like to see you access in your life through this Adventure.

● **Commit** yourself to this Adventure. Take it seriously. If you give it some time and attention, you'll be rolling in the payoff. Check it out for a few days, and then try to get solid before the first week is over.

● **Honesty** is the best policy. Be brutally honest with yourself—and with God—as you answer the questions in this journal.

● **Relax.** If you miss a day, don't go crazy trying to make it up. Just get going on the current day. Later you can go back and see what you missed.

● **Connect** with others. Try doing this Adventure with a few friends or your youth group. You can keep tabs on each other and pool new ideas and support.

● **Prepare** yourself by taking a look at the journal now, especially pages 5–14. See what's coming up. During the Adventure you'll take five action steps. Some may be fairly basic and familiar; others involve more prep. But don't worry! Every week the BackCheck/Coming Attractions pages will help you keep on track.

The outside of each daily page has a place for the date (on the arrow pointing down). Take a second now to locate a calendar. Find the Sunday you plan to begin the Adventure. Write that date on Sunday, Day 1 (p. 19). Then write the dates, in order, on all the pages that follow.

● **Expect** to grow. Great things can happen as you do this Adventure. God moves in powerful ways when people let him. He can make a big difference in *your* life, too.

● **Ask questions.** Don't expect to get all the info on your own. There may be some things that just don't make sense. At the bottom of each daily page there is a space to write down your unanswered questions—what you don't know, don't understand, or just don't get. Don't write these down and toss them. Try to get them answered—do some research on your own, ask someone who might know, or talk about these questions in your youth group or at church.

● **Spend some extra time.** Each week read a chapter in the Adventure Guidebook *When the Troops Are Tired* by Dr. David Mains. This book will give you the 411 on all eight of the Adventure PowerPoints and the action steps you will be tackling every day. (See p. 18.)

● **Get the bonus.** Keep track of the Bible passages that really hit home. And then get memorizing. God's Word will go farther to power you up in your bean than on the shelf.

THE POWERPOINTS

DURING THE NEXT 50 days, this journal will focus on eight PowerPoints that will help you access God's power for your life.

● PowerPoint 1: Good Grief.
The bad things of life often lead to powerfully good changes.

● PowerPoint 2: 24/7 Church.
God's work doesn't end at the church door. He's open all night, all week.

● PowerPoint 3: Common Grounds.
Going it alone is a sure way to fail. Reach out to others and combine your spiritual power.

● PowerPoint 4: Back Talk.
There are probably several people who care for your spiritual needs: pastor, youth leader, teachers, parents. But have you ever told them *what* you need?

● PowerPoint 5: Fast Times.
It's an amazingly powerful thing to give up food to focus on prayer.

● PowerPoint 6: Telling Secrets.
What is God doing in your life? Don't keep it a secret; power up others and yourself by letting the word get out.

● PowerPoint 7: Cross Purposes.
Do you know who the Christians are around you (not just the ones in your church or youth group)? You don't have to agree on every detail, but if they follow the crucified Christ, you're on the same home page.

● PowerPoint 8: Power Up.
The resurrection of Jesus was God's all-time awesome display of power. He says that same power now lives in us!

And the five action steps will be a way for you to turn on the power in your life.

ADVENTURE PREVIEW

As you get farther into the Adventure, you can refer back to this list for a brief review of the action steps and how often you're to do each one. (For a more complete description of the action steps, see pp. 7–14.) Don't worry about keeping everything in your head. This journal will remind you of all your assignments on the BackCheck/Coming Attractions pages.

EVERY DAY
● **Read** the assigned Bible passages and answer the questions in the journal.

● **Take it to the top** by praying the "Good Grief" Prayer using the words on page 8 as a guide (Action Step 1, pp. 7–8).

● **Take a 24/7 check** and record how God did something **To** you or worked **Through** you at some point during the day (Action Step 2, p. 9).

EVERY WEEK
● **Read** the chapter in Dr. David Mains' book *When the Troops Are Tired*.

● **Talk about it!** Share your 24/7 experiences with someone (Action Step 2, p. 9).

ONCE
● **Send out invitations** by sharing your hospitality with others (Action Step 3, p. 10).

● **Give someone a piece of your mind** and let your pastor or youth leader know what's hot or not in your life (Action Step 4, p. 12).

● **Get hungry** and go without food for a few moments to concentrate on some serious prayer (Action Step 5, p. 13).

BONUS
● **Store some power.** Try memorizing some of the Bible verses as you go along.

Take It to the Top
EVERY DAY

AcTioN StEp 1

THEY CALL IT MARCH MADNESS. It's the best of college basketball: 64 teams grappling for the championship. But the first round always offers some pretty unlikely matchups. You're likely to see Podunk State College, champs of the Grapefruit League, go up against a traditional powerhouse like Kansas, Kentucky, or Duke.

Once in a while, these games get exciting. Somewhere late in the first half, Podunk drains a few threes and steals the lead. Suddenly they smell UPSET. *We can do it!* They start thinking they can win, and all of a sudden they're full of energy. With the crowd rooting for David to slay Goliath, the upstarts may even keep the lead till halftime.

But the dream doesn't last long. Usually the Goliath team starts the second half with a couple of monster-dunks. Then some steals or offensive rebounds, and the refs make a questionable call or two. Now the Podunk players are whining, bickering, and worrying. They're playing their hearts out, but the other team is taller, stronger, quicker. *We just can't win,* the underdogs tell themselves. There may be ten minutes to go, but their heads are hanging—they're already defeated.

There's a spiritual lesson in this story somewhere, but I forget what it is. Oh, yes, here we go. . . . We often get defeated spiritually by our own attitudes. Bad things happen to us, and we get depressed. *We just can't win,* we tell ourselves, and in the process we let our misfortunes lead us away from God rather than toward him.

And that leads us away from God's power to change things.

I'm not talking about "positive thinking"—*just thinking rosy thoughts*—but about **positive praying.** You see, no matter how difficult things are for you, God has power to change things . . . and he has power to change *you.* Sure, God can turn bad situations to good ones, but he can also make you a stronger person as you deal with the hard times.

So stop dragging that frown on the floor. Take it to the top—in prayer—and see what miracles God is going to perform for you and through you and in you.

WhaT2Do: Once a day, pray the "Good Grief" Prayer on the next page. You can put it in your own words, but try to follow this basic pattern, filling in the blank space with whatever problem is getting you down. And don't just launch this prayer to God; take time to listen for his response, too.

Note: Don't forget the bonus idea of memorizing the Bible verses that spark your interest. It's a great way to keep it at the top.

The "Good Grief" Prayer

Lord,

I'm trying to "**power up**" by relying on your strength.

But right now I'm concerned about:

_____

[fill in a problem you're concerned about].

I know that you can turn this grief to **good** in some

amazing way.

I'm counting on you to work for me, through me, and in me.

Keep reminding me of what you're up to.

And thanks for the **miracles** you've already done

in my life.

Amen.

Take a 24/7 Check
EVERY DAY
AcTioN StEp 2

"YES, MR. PRINCIPAL, you have every reason to suspect me of setting off those nuclear devices in the physics lab, but I know you're wise enough to see that I'm too nice to do anything so destructive."

You probably know some smooth operator who gets out of jams by sweet-talking parents, teachers, principals, or cops. But how does this person talk when those authorities turn their backs?

"Ha, I sure fooled them!"

"My parents are clueless."

"I played that principal like a Fender bass."

Sometimes these people are so slick that you admire their talent—but eventually you begin to wonder what they're saying when *your* back is turned. If they lie to the others to get their way, what makes you think *you* can trust what they say?

Sadly, many Christians play the same kind of game with God. They're all holy hallelujah in church, but half a week later God seems like a distant memory. They have the right answers in youth group, but the rest of the week they act as if Jesus doesn't exist. There's something wrong with that.

Character is what you are when no one's looking. If you're a Christian, then be a Christian—24 hours a day, 7 days a week. You'll find that God is a 24/7 God, too. He'll be there for you nonstop. As you begin to see God in your life beyond the church services, you'll realize the phenomenal power that's available to you every day of the week.

WhaT2Do: Each day of the Adventure, do the 3TC—the Three-T Check—and record your findings on pages 40–41. It should take only 5–10 minutes, or maybe a little longer.

1. To. Ask yourself, "How did God get through *to* me today?" This could be an answer to prayer, an idea you got from reading the Bible, or a helpful conversation with a friend . . . anything God did to crash through your skull.

2. Through. Ask yourself, "How did God work *through* me today?" Did God use you to encourage someone else? How did God help you to live out your faith today?

3. Talk about it! As you fill in the To and Through parts of the chart, think about telling someone else about what's happening. How can you let others know about the power that's working to and through you? You might start with family members or close Christian friends, but you may also find that it's a great way to start sharing your faith with non-Christians. Try to *talk about* your 24/7 experiences at least once each week.

Review: Every day you'll be turning to the handy chart (pp. 40–41) for your 3TC. It may take a while for you to start recognizing the 24/7 miracles happening *to* and *through* you, but keep at it. You'll improve with practice. Then, at least once a week during the Adventure, *talk about* some of your 3TCs with someone.

Send Out Invitations
ONCE
AcTioN
StEp 3

DID YOU HAVE a clubhouse as a kid? Someplace you and your playmates could go to get away from the hustle and bustle of elementary-school life? Some kids were lucky enough to have tree houses or "forts"; others just gathered a group in their rec room or bedroom. The specific place didn't matter so much, as long as the group members felt "at home."

Well, you've graduated from your clubhouse days, but you may still have a special place. A pizza joint, a mall, the band room, a ball field, the sidewalk in front of 7-Eleven. You feel comfortable there—but why? It's not the ambiance of the place, the furniture or linoleum, *you just feel that you* **belong**.

The Bible talks about the "gift of hospitality," an ability to make people feel at home. People with this gift regularly open their homes to friends and strangers alike, sharing the resources God has given them. While some people have a special knack for it, *all* Christians are invited to show hospitality to some extent.

But what if you don't own a home? And what if your folks don't let you invite the lacrosse team over after school? You can still express hospitality by making people feel at home *wherever you are*—in the school cafeteria or the Pizza Hut. You can "send out invitations" to those around you, but we're not talking about golden lettering and RSVPs. You send out an invitation every time you greet someone with a smile, whenever you ask about his or her life, whenever you open your heart to someone who needs a friend. Create your own "clubhouse" by sharing the open heart of Jesus.

WhaT2Do: Start by thinking about how you could open up your home—perhaps your room or your yard—for God's purposes. Ask God to give you ideas. Could you start an after-school prayer group with your friends? Could your family sort of "adopt" a friend of yours whose parents seem to always be too busy? Or could your family invite a single-parent family along on some of your activities? (Note: "God's purposes" can involve people-helping as well as prayer and Bible study.)

Naturally, you'll need to talk things over with your folks. If they are also doing this Adventure, you can work together on this step (but you may need to encourage them to really go for it, doing something that makes a difference). Even if they're not on the Adventure, they may cooperate with you on this step. Let them help work out the details.

What if you're not allowed to open your home to others? Then you have to get creative. Ask God for *more* ideas about how to "send out invitations" to people at school or in the neighborhood. How can you make them feel at home with you and with God?

Maybe you can find a neutral site. Talk with your youth director about getting together at church, or maybe you could meet people at a restaurant, or why not hold a prayer meeting in some corner of the mall? Feel free to work together with another adventurer on this step.

If you surf the Web, think about this: How can you use the Internet for God's purposes? Can you start a "virtual clubhouse," in which people will chat about God? Even if you don't own your own home, it's getting pretty easy to set up a "home page." Think about it.

What if you're terrified about this whole process? *What can I say? I'm terrible at witnessing to people! Just talking to people gives me the jitters.*

Relax. Please understand that we're not telling you to "witness." We're asking you to open your heart to others. (In the process you can't help but *be* a witness, but you don't have to try too hard.) Be yourself. You don't have to impress anyone. Just show interest in the other people you're dealing with.

And if you're drawing a blank, here are some questions you might ask people:

- What's your favorite subject in school, and why?
- What would you like to be doing ten years from now?
- If you got a free plane ticket to any place in the world, where would you like to go, and why?
- Tell me about one day from your childhood that you'd like to live over again.
- How real is God in your life?

Note: We're not talking about entertaining or throwing great parties for your friends. We're really talking about making people feel welcome and wanted. You can help the people around you feel like they belong—whether it's at church, school, or the skate shop. And in the process you'll feel more like you belong also.

Give Someone a Piece of Your Mind.
ONCE
AcTioN StEp 4

REPORT CARDS. Do you love them or hate them? Depends on your grades, right?

But when you think about it, your report card actually helps you more when it's bad. Sure, a few D's and F's may get you grounded or kick you out of extracurricular activities, but those grades are also telling you something very important. *You're not getting it! Work harder! Study more!*

Imagine a school with no report cards. You take tests, grades are compiled, but no one tells you what they are. And then when you're ready to apply for college it's "Surprise! Here's your GPA."

Churches can be like that. As long as everyone just smiles and says polite things, no one will have any idea of how it's really going. If your youth group is talking about issues that don't matter to you, you need to say something—or else it will just keep on happening. Teachers and preachers need to know when they're on target and when not.

Naturally, you prefer getting good grades. And when you get praised for doing well, that makes you want to continue. The same goes for your church leaders. Don't complain; look for things you can praise.

Of course, you could be wrong. So maintain a humble attitude as you offer your feedback, but don't let that keep you from speaking up. Your pastor, church school teachers, and youth leaders can make your Christian life more effective—if you help them to be as effective as they can be.

WhaT2Do: Start by PRAYING. For the first three weeks of the Adventure, make it a point to pray for your youth leader (or you could choose your pastor or church school teacher instead). Pray before *and during* each meeting. But pray also for yourself, that you will hear God's message to you during this time.

Then, ACT on what you learn. During those first three weeks, make a special effort to put your leader's words (and God's words) into action. Think about how this message is changing your life.

You don't have to stop all of this in the fourth week—these are great habits to hang on to—but now it's time for something else. Between the fourth week and the end of the Adventure, WRITE A LETTER (or e-mail) to your youth leader. This is an opportunity for you to offer ideas about your life and what you need.

Here are some thoughts you might share:
- This is one way that you've influenced my life . . .
- This is something you said that has really helped me . . .
- It would be helpful to me if you could speak about . . .

Remember: Complaints aren't the best way to get through to someone. It's best to let people know what they are doing well. Try to be positive and practical in your feedback. But make sure you're honest and tell your leader what your real needs are and what the world you live in is really like.

Get Hungry

ONCE

ACTION STEP 5

"**H**AVE A COOKIE, Dan."

"Can't."

"Oh, come on. Just one!"

"Nope. I have to make weight tomorrow."

Dan is a wrestler. If he weighs in even a half-pound above the limit, he can't compete in that match. That cookie could mean a championship.

You have to give these guys credit. Wrestlers are so dedicated to their sport that they observe a strict diet in order to gain strength without gaining weight. They know what they want, and even food won't lure them away.

The Bible says that Christians are in a wrestling match, too, but not against human opponents. We struggle in prayer against the "evil rulers and authorities of the unseen world" (Ephesians 6:12). How dedicated are we? Are we willing to go without food for a while to concentrate on prayer?

Many people in the Bible and throughout history have done exactly that. It's called *fasting*—giving up food for a period of time to focus on God. There's nothing magical in it, as if our hunger pangs force God into action. But it does show God (and ourselves) that we mean business. And we're not saying that there's something wrong with food. When you break your fast, you can feast with joy. But fasting is a way of showing that our love for God is even more important than food. If wrestlers can do it for a mere sport, why can't we?

WhaT2Do: Fast at least once during the Adventure. (And we're not talking about "fast food.") You have several options. Choose a plan that fits your health and spiritual needs, and stick to it. Make sure you consult a parent and inform him or her of your intentions.

1. The lunch fast. Instead of chowing down on the mystery meat in your school cafeteria, take time for prayer instead. If you can do this with a group of Christian friends at school, great! Or go it alone, but don't make a big show of it. Also you could try this on a weekend, when you can set aside some serious midday time for prayer.

2. The lunch-to-lunch juice fast. Eat a healthy meal, including fruits and vegetables, for lunch one day. Then skip supper and breakfast (make sure you drink plenty of water and fruit juices—but not too much citrus). Break your fast joyfully with another healthy lunch (but don't pig out; you'll get sick). This two-meal fast could also go breakfast-to-breakfast or supper-to-supper, but the midday option is probably the easiest.

Yo! There are some health risks involved in fasting, so be careful. If you are pregnant, diabetic, or hypoglycemic, or if you have other health problems, it's best not to try a food fast. If you have any history of an eating disorder or

depression, don't do this fast unless your doctor okays everything. If you have any questions at all, see your doctor first. We are not recommending longer fasts without consulting a doctor, your parents, and your youth leader (or another church leader). A day at a time is plenty.

If you cannot (or should not) embark on a food fast, we offer another option that can be just as powerful:

3. The replacement fast. Find some other habit that is nearly as central to your life as food: watching TV, playing computer games, surfing the Net, talking on the phone, shopping. This does not have to be a bad habit (just as eating is not a bad thing), but it's something you will choose to give up for a certain period of time so that you can focus on God.

Remember: The purpose of fasting is to draw closer to God, putting him above even your most basic needs. So use those hunger pangs and withdrawal symptoms to spark thoughts of God's presence. Take your normal eating (or whatever you're replacing) time to study the Bible or to listen for God's whispers. Don't take pride in how much weight you're losing and don't brag about this as some major spiritual accomplishment. Don't push yourself beyond what God enables you to do, and don't get legalistic with yourself about what you may or may not eat or drink. All of that is just distraction. Use this occasion to "power up"—to get on God's wavelength.

PowerUP
Kicking Your Faith to a New Level

Read Psalm 30.

It's a remarkable affirmation that God uses good times and bad times to complete his work in us.

1. What, according to David, is the result of calling to the Lord for help?

2. List the situations in your life in which you wish God would help you.

3. What is the one situation you listed above that is the most important or pressing?

4. What would you ask God to do to help you or power you up in this situation?

     ❑ Just make it all better

❑ I could use a little more strength

     ❑ If I had closer friends it wouldn't be so bad

         ❑ How about listening to my prayers

   ❑ Winning the lottery would make it seem a whole lot better

      ❑ As long as you know what you're doing, I'm game

5. How do you think God could use this situation?

Read Acts 12:1-19a.

This passage describes a wild time when the followers of Jesus experienced great things from God and violent opposition from people in power.

1. Write a real quick summary of this passage.

2. God turned this bad situation into a good one at a time when the early church was in a bad way. Write a story about the situation that you mentioned yesterday in which God does a turnaround like that for you.

3. How can God help you kick your faith to the next level?

4. Skim the different theme introductions in the journal (look at the Table of Contents for an easy way to find right where to go). What PowerPoints in this Adventure seem valuable to you?

❏ Good Grief   ❏ 24/7 Church
     ❏ Common Grounds   ❏ Back Talk
❏ Fast Times   ❏ Telling Secrets
     ❏ Cross Purposes   ❏ Power Up

POWERPOINT
1

Good Grief

"LIFE IS HARD and then you die."

You may have seen a T-shirt or poster with that cheery comment, or some variation of it. And if you're in the middle of a painful breakup, a losing season, or a family that doesn't understand you, you may feel the same way. Pop quizzes, younger siblings, fickle friends, impossibly thin supermodels, raging hormones, acne, and the opposite sex, in general, all conspire to make you miserable.

We all become a bit like Charlie Brown, that round-headed guy in the comics who just can't win for losing. "Good grief," he says whenever his dog outsmarts him, his teacher insults him, or his center fielder tries to catch a fly ball with her head. "Good grief."

Those two words sum up the Bible's teaching on the subject. We will have grief in this life, no doubt about it. We will always identify with Job, the guy who lost everything and sat on his ash pile wondering why. "Here on earth you will have many trials and sorrows," Jesus said (John 16:33).

But he didn't stop there. "Take heart," he added, "because I have overcome the world." Grief can, in fact, be good. In his famous Sermon on the Mount, Jesus said, "God blesses those who mourn" (Matthew 5:4).

"We can rejoice," the apostle Paul wrote, "when we run into problems and trials, for we know that they are good for us." Good for us? How? The text goes on to tell us that, by enduring hard times, we develop character, and we learn to depend on God to help us (Romans 5:3–5).

Take Joseph. Sold into slavery by his jealous brothers, he became the best slave in his household—until he was falsely accused of trying to rape the boss's wife. Thrown in prison, he became an assistant to the warden. His knack for interpreting dreams came to the attention of the king of Egypt, who eventually made him second in command.

Lots of bad things happened to Joseph, but he never got defeated. Trusting in God, he made the best of each bad situation. After his brothers came to buy grain from Joseph's storehouses, Joseph told them, "As far as I am concerned, God turned into good what you meant for evil" (Genesis 50:20).

Many Christians these days are complainers, moaning about this world's downhill slide, griping about how tough it is to be a Christian. But complaining saps your energy, robs you of power. Instead of looking at how bad everything is, rejoice that you can trust in God to bring something good out of it all.

You don't have to wear rose-colored glasses or deny the existence of evil in this world. You just have to expect God to act. Maybe God will change the situation. Maybe God will change *you*. How will he display his awesome power? And how can you tap into it?

BaCkCheCk
BaCkCheCk

Check the box if you have completed the assignment.

- ☐ I read introductory pages 3–14.
- ☐ I read the introduction in *When the Troops Are Tired*.
- ☐ I did the Warm-Up days on pages 15 and 16.
- ☐ I read page 17 (Good Grief).

ComiNg AttRacTioNs

PowerPoint 1: Good Grief

Daily Assignments:
- Read the assigned Bible passages and answer the questions in the journal.
- Pray the "Good Grief" Prayer (Action Step 1, pp. 7–8).
- Take a 24/7 check on pages 40–41 (Action Step 2, p. 9).

Assignments for this week:
- Read chapter 1 in *When the Troops Are Tired*.
- Talk about a 24/7 experience to someone at least once this week (Action Step 2, p. 9).
- Bonus: Memorize the Bible verses that power you up.

Still to Come:
- Send out invitations (Action Step 3, p. 10).
- Give someone a piece of your mind (Action Step 4, p. 12).
- Get hungry (Action Step 5, p. 13).

Get the 411 on this 50-Day Adventure:
When the Troops Are Tired by Dr. David Mains (Guidebook or Audio Guidebook)

In addition to your journal read the Adventure Guidebook. This essential, easy-to-read book includes a chapter for each of the eight Adventure PowerPoints. You'll get:
- Extra info, insights, and inspiration.
- Practical helps and stories.
- In-depth explanations.

Pocket the Pack: *The Tapped-Out Christian's Energy Pack*

This handy pack gives you a way to keep God's Word at your fingertips 24/7. It includes 23 verses that relate specifically to the Adventure PowerPoints. You'll also find this pack invaluable for helping you with the bonus idea of memorizing Bible verses.

Read Ruth 1:1-22; 4:13-17.

1. If you made a movie of chapter 1, what kind of movie would it be? Briefly explain.

2. How did things change for Naomi (and Ruth) by chapter 4?

3. Naomi took a new name (Ruth 1:20) because things were going so bad for her. If you adopted a new name to reflect how things are going for you these days, what would it be?

4. Ruth and her sister-in-law Orpah both lost their husbands. How did they deal with their grief differently?

5. What was Ruth's "good grief"?

Monday/Date

Read Acts 8:1b-4; 11:19-21.

1. How do you think the early believers felt about being persecuted?

2. Keep it clean, but what names do you think the Christians were calling Saul, their chief persecutor?

3. What was the result of the scattering of the church?

4. If persecution suddenly came upon your church or youth group, and you all had to leave the country, where do you think people would go? (Put stars on the map below.)

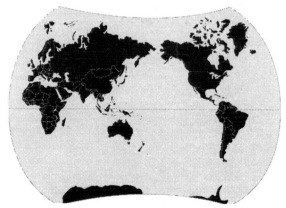

5. What effect do you think this would have on the people in those nations where you'd go?

Read James 1:1-8.

1. According to these verses, why are trials good for us?

2. How do you think the original readers reacted to these verses?
"Well, James,

_____

_____ ."

3. What trials have you faced in the last year?

4. How have they helped you become "strong and ready" ("mature and complete"—NIV)?

❏ My IQ tripled

    ❏ I learned to trust God more

        ❏ My hair turned prematurely gray

           ❏ I learned something about human nature

      ❏ I'll do better next time

    ❏ Sales clerks started offering me senior citizen discounts

❏ I saw God turn something bad to something good

      ❏ I don't know—I don't see it yet

❏ Other _____

5. How would you describe "good grief" to your best friend?

Wednesday Date

Read 1 Timothy 1:12-17.

Paul writes to oppose false teachers who want people to live under Jewish law instead of Christian grace. Paul is Exhibit A of God's goodness to people who don't deserve it.

1. On Day 2, we read of Paul (then known as Saul) persecuting Christians. As he writes this in 1 Timothy, what does he think of those old days?

2. How does he explain his turnaround?

3. What's the most amazing personal transformation you've ever seen?

4. Is this saying that there's a good side to sin? If so, what is it?

5. Let's say you've committed lots of sins in the past, and you're ashamed of it all. According to today's scripture, what kind of attitude should you have about that? (Check all you agree with.)
❏ Who cares?   ❏ It really wasn't that bad
          ❏ It's past, it's forgiven, I'm free
❏ Praise God! My transformation is a testimony to his phenomenal grace
          ❏ Let me go back and sin some more, so God can show more grace

Read Judges 7:1–25.

The Israelites are on a roller coaster ride with God: God blesses them, and they're high. They forget God and they drop like a rock. "Oh, we're sorry!" they say. "Help us!" And God ramps them back up again. God called an ordinary man named Gideon when they were at the bottom.

1. How many soldiers did Gideon start with? How many did he end up with?

2. How do you think Gideon felt when God told him to go into battle with so few men (see verse 7)?

3. Imagine, though, what the Midianites were thinking when, in the middle of the night, they saw bright lights and heard trumpets. What might have been going through their minds?

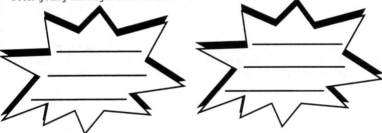

4. Has it ever seemed to you that God took away a resource you needed to live a good life that would glorify him?
❏ Good grades?   ❏ Money?   ❏ A job?
          ❏ A relationship?
                    ❏ A particular ability you wish you had?
❏ Good health?   ❏ Other _____

5. In light of Gideon's story, why might God do that?

Friday Date

Read John 11:1-44.

1. How did Martha and Mary feel about their brother's death?

2. What do you think Martha was thinking in verses 21–27?

3. According to verse 4, why did Lazarus get sick?

4. Has God ever been glorified by "bad" things that have happened to you?

5. One company has a slogan that says it "brings good things to life." According to verse 25, we could say the same thing about Jesus, but why don't you come up with a different slogan for Jesus' life-giving powers?

6. In your own words, briefly explain what "good grief" is all about.

24/7 Church

IT PROBABLY STARTED with comic books.

Some good character, perhaps even the hero, was accused of a terrible crime. All the evidence pointed straight to him, but how could this honest person do such a dastardly deed?

Not to fear, good readers. It wasn't our hero at all, but his *evil twin*.

How convenient. And what a great excuse! "No, Mr. Vice Principal, that wasn't me locking all the teachers in the teacher's lounge. It was that evil twin of mine." (NOTE: This won't work with your parents. They would know if you have an evil twin or not.)

Too many Christians have "evil twins." Or maybe it's the other way around: they have a "righteous twin" who worships in church on Sunday, but they live the rest of the week as if God didn't matter.

Jesus hated it when people did that. He called them "whitewashed tombs"— really pretty on the outside, but full of inner decay (Matthew 23:27). He quoted an Old Testament verse: "These people honor me with their lips, but their hearts are far away" (Matthew 15:8). God isn't fooled by your sweet-talking in church if you don't back it up with everyday commitment. He doesn't fall for that "righteous twin" act.

Does that mean you shouldn't go to church if you're not perfect? Of course not. God knows you struggle with various temptations, and he enjoys the company of all his struggling worshipers. But we need to make a *connection* between the church service and the rest of our lives. Our worship needs to thrust us out into our communities with a renewed commitment to follow Jesus 24 hours a day, 7 days a week. You can't hang up your halo on the way out of the church lobby. Your Christian faith needs to be a nonstop, everyday thing.

Does that mean you have to stay busy all the time, always praying or reading the Bible, always witnessing, always making little arts and crafts objects to send to missionaries in Honduras? Well, no. You just need to . . . I don't know how else to say it: you need to hang with God. Shoot silent sentence prayers to him throughout the day. Listen for his advice in the situations you face. Think about how God feels when you're deciding what to do. Enjoy the beauty all around you as a gift from God. Count on his strength to get you through tough times. Rest in him. Thank him.

"Whatever you do or say," the Bible says, "let it be as a representative of the Lord Jesus" (Colossians 3:17). The fact is, God is there for you 24/7. Any time, day or night, you can call on him. No busy signals. No call waiting. He wants you to be there for him, too.

So what are you going to do about that "twin" now?

BaCkCheCk
BaCkCheCk

Check the box if you have completed the assignment.

❏ I read chapter 1 in *When the Troops Are Tired*.
❏ I did Days 1–6.
❏ I prayed the "Good Grief" Prayer (p. 8).
❏ I took a 24/7 check on pages 40–41 (Action Step 2, p.9).
❏ I talked about my 24/7 experiences once this week to someone (Action Step 2, p. 9).
❏ I have read page 25 (24/7 Church).
❏ I memorized a Bible verse this week (Bonus).

PowerPoint 2: 24/7 Church

Daily Assignments:
● Read the assigned Bible passages and answer the questions in the journal.
● Pray the "Good Grief" Prayer (Action Step 1, pp. 7–8).
● Take a 24/7 check on pages 40–41 (Action Step 2, p. 9).

Assignments for this week:
● Read chapter 2 in *When the Troops Are Tired*.
● Talk about a 24/7 experience to someone at least once this week (Action Step 2, p. 9).
● Bonus: Memorize the Bible verses that power you up.
● Don't forget to pray for your youth leader (Action Step 4, p. 12).

Still to Come:
● Send out invitations (Action Step 3, p. 10).
● Give someone a piece of your mind (Action Step 4, p. 12).
● Get hungry (Action Step 5, p. 13).

Read Daniel 6:1-28.

Daniel attracted trouble like a lightning rod. People loved him because God gave him so much wisdom. They hated him for the same reason.

1. How often did Daniel kneel and pray in his room?

2. Why do you think the windows were opened (verse 10)?
❑ So everyone could see him praying and know how righteous he was
❑ It got hot in Persia before air conditioning was invented
❑ To let out the fumes from the incense Daniel was burning
❑ So Daniel could face Jerusalem and be reminded of God's plans for his people
❑ In the original language, it really means he was running Win95 and surfing the Net

3. How did the decree change Daniel's behavior?

4. You're probably not dealing with any decrees from Persian kings, but what pressures do you feel *not* to practice your faith or pray in your daily life?

5. Daniel faced hungry lions—and was spared. What kinds of "lions" would you face if you went ahead and lived like a Christian 24/7—and how would God rescue you?

Monday Date

Read Luke 19:1-10.

It doesn't take a genius to understand why a crooked tax collector doesn't get invited to a lot of parties.

1. Zacchaeus was a tax collector—a profession despised by most Jews in that day. What kinds of people are generally despised today?

2. How do you think Zack felt when Jesus invited himself over?

3. What did Zack promise to do after spending time with Jesus?

4. There's a simple point here: Jesus makes a difference in people's lives. Pick a TV character you're familiar with—for instance, someone on "Friends" or "Party of Five." How would Jesus make a difference in that person's life?

5. How has Jesus changed your life?

6. You know what happens when your best friend finally gets a boyfriend or girlfriend—they're together during lunch, after school, and every Friday night. It seems like they're together 24/7. Now a lot of people are like that when they first meet Jesus, but the trick is to keep it that way. So, what ideas do you have about your 24/7 relationship with Jesus now?

Read Proverbs 31:10-31.

1. What are five things the "virtuous wife" does that you find most impressive in this passage?

2. List at least one quality or activity from this chapter that you also see in . . .

Your mother or father: _____

Yourself: _____

Any other family member. Name _____

_____

3. Verse 28 says that this woman's children bless her. When was the last time you blessed your mom (or dad)?

4. If this chapter became an article in *Seventeen* magazine, what would the title be?

5. When does this woman get any rest? In what ways do you think she is a 24/7 Christian?

6. Has taking 24/7 checks every day (Action Step 2) helped you to realize God's involvement in your life throughout the day better? How 'bout *your* involvement with God throughout the day?

Read Deuteronomy 6:1-9.

1. According to these verses, what happens if you keep God's commandments?

2. Write a list of all the different ways God commanded the Israelites to be his 24/7 followers.

3. Verse 7 talks about sitting at home and walking along the road. If you were to rewrite this for your kind of life, what activities would you list? Talk about God's words when . . .
❏ You're roller blading
    ❏ The vice principal is yelling at you
        ❏ You and your friends are just hanging

Now add your own.

4. At what time of the week do you act most like a Christian?

How about least like a Christian?

5. In what place do you act most like a Christian?

And least like a Christian?

6. How can you ensure you'll hear God when he wants to get a message through?

Read Ephesians 6:5-9.

Starting in chapter five, verse 21, Paul has the same message for husbands and wives, parents and children, masters and slaves: "Submit to one another out of reverence for Christ."

1. What difference would it make for a slave to be a 24/7 Christian?

2. Obviously, this was written for a time in which slavery was part of the culture, but let's try to apply it to our day. What "masters" do you have? What people have control over what you do?

3. How would your behavior change if you served your earthly "masters" as if you were serving Christ?

4. Verse 7 says we should "work with enthusiasm." Can you find a new way to say that?

5. You probably don't think of yourself as a "master," but you probably have some influence on *somebody,* even a younger sibling or a good friend. Name one or two people you influence.

6. How would you treat them differently if you followed verse 9?

Friday Date

Read Colossians 4:2-6.

1. What does the apostle Paul (who wrote this) want people to pray for?

2. What does it mean to "live wisely among those who are not Christians" (verse 5)?

3. What salty foods do you like? What does salt do for those foods?

4. How can your behavior be "salty" to someone else?

5. What questions might someone ask that you need to know how to answer?

6. What in the world does this have to do with being a 24/7 Christian?

POWERPOINT 3

Common Grounds

THEY SAY COFFEE is bad for you—it rots your gut and wires your nerves—but for millions of people, there's nothing quite like it. Take it black or what New Yorkers call "regular" (cream and sugar), straight or flavored, strong or stronger, espresso, cappuccino, mocha, or latte. Coffee houses sprouted like crazy in Seattle, blossoming a whole new cultural/musical style, and now the coffee craze is sweeping the world. Starbucks is setting up shop in every other building.

Coffee was always a solitary drink, a don't-bother-me-I'm-not-awake-yet elixir. But now it's a social thing. People get together "over a cup of coffee" to make deals and swap stories. And coffee houses bring strangers together in their common love of music and the sweet scent of Colombian roast. Some churches have been doing this for decades—inviting folks to hang around after the service for the "coffee hour," offering acid-burn liquid from those tin cylinders to wash down stale coffee cake. Who'd have thought they'd be so trendy?

I (Randy) have a theory about this. Yes, I've spent hours sipping house blend, mulling over this social development. Ready? Here it is: *Coffee creates a home.*

Think about it. Lots of people these days are "homeless," and I'm not talking about walking the street. People have lost their roots. Even if they have houses and families. People are desperate to "go home," wherever that home might be.

But you hear the perking of a coffee maker or catch a whiff of that brew, and suddenly you feel at home. The people you're with are "family."

Christians should be like coffee. We should be creating "home" for people wherever we go. When the psalmist says "God is our refuge" (Psalm 46:1), what is he saying? *God is our home.*

Sure, Jesus said he was going to get some heavenly mansions ready for our arrival (John 14:2), but he also said that, *here on earth,* God's kingdom was about a runaway son *coming home* to his loving dad (Luke 15:11–32).

We carry that "home" around with us, wherever we go, and we can share it with everyone we meet. Talk about the homey scent of coffee! The Bible says we are "a fragrance presented by Christ" (2 Corinthians 2:15). One of the most important gifts in the early church was hospitality, as Christians opened their homes to others. Traveling preachers were always roaming the Roman Empire, and they needed places to crash. Sometimes new Christians would be kicked out of their non-Christian homes, and they'd need faithful families to take them in. Even during times of persecution, Christians became known as people who would care for the sick, feed the hungry, or take in the wanderer. Home sweet home.

As a student, you may be limited in the type of hospitality you can offer. It's your parents' home, really. But you can carry this sense of "home" with you throughout the day. Look around you. See your friends and classmates who desperately need a place of peace. You can offer them a listening ear, an understanding heart, a cup of coffee . . . a home away from home.

BaCkCheCk
BaCkCheCk

Check the box if you have completed the assignment.

❑ I read chapter 2 in *When the Troops Are Tired*.
❑ I did Days 7–13.
❑ I prayed the "Good Grief" Prayer (p. 8).
❑ I took a 24/7 check on pages 40–41 (p. 9).
❑ I talked about my 24/7 experiences once this week to someone (p. 9).
❑ I read page 33 (Common Grounds).
❑ I memorized a Bible verse this week (Bonus).

PowerPoint 3: Common Grounds

Daily Assignments:
● Read the assigned Bible passages and answer the questions in the journal.
● Pray the "Good Grief" Prayer (p. 8).
● Take a 24/7 check on pages 40–41 (p. 9).

Assignments for this week:
● Read chapter 3 in *When the Troops Are Tired*.
● Talk about a 24/7 experience to someone at least once this week (p. 9).
● Bonus: Memorize the Bible verses that power you up.
● Don't forget to pray for your youth leader (Action Step 4, p. 12).

Before the End:
● Send out invitations (Action Step 3, p. 10).

Still to Come:
● Give someone a piece of your mind (Action Step 4, p. 12).
● Get hungry (Action Step 5, p. 13).

Read Luke 10:38-42.

1. If this story occurred on "Home Improvement," how would it go?

2. What kind of hospitality did Martha show? What kind did Mary show?

3. Are you more like Martha or more like Mary, a doer or a listener? Do you like to do stuff with others or just sit around and talk?

4. Martha's problem was not so much the work she was doing, but the fact that she dissed Mary. There are different ways of showing hospitality. You may not be able to invite all your acquaintances over for a five-course dinner, but how *can* you find common grounds and help make them feel at home?

Monday Date

Read 1 Timothy 3:1-7; 5:9-10.

1. What is the "good she has done" mentioned in chapter 5?

2. One major theme of 1 Timothy is the organization of the church. But we also see in these job descriptions how people lived out their faith. As you think over your actions of the past week, what did you do to make other people think that you're a Christian?

3. Notice how important the home is for the elder in chapter 3 and the widow in chapter 5. What ideas can you draw from these verses about how to make others feel at home?

4. You and your friends must have one place (or more) where you feel at home—your common ground. What can you do to invite others to your common ground and help them to feel at home there also?

Read 1 Peter 4:7-11.

1. What does it mean to be "earnest and disciplined"? How can you be this way?

2. "Love covers a multitude of sins." That's a huge statement. What does it mean?

3. These verses talk about using our various gifts. Yet it's interesting that there's no *if* attached to hospitality. We're all supposed to show it, but we may do so in different ways. How can you use your unique gifts to make others feel at home?

4. To whom should you show love?
- ❏ Nice people   ❏ Good-looking people   ❏ Drug addicts
- ❏ People who love you   ❏ Popular kids at school
- ❏ People with a lot of pierced body parts
- ❏ Prisoners   ❏ Your parents   ❏ Homosexuals
- ❏ Your youth leader   ❏ People with money

5. One of the places that should be "common ground" for us all is church. But that is not always the case. What ideas do you have that could help your church or youth group become "common grounds" for others in your school or community who could really use a place to hang their hat?

**Wednesday
Date**

Read 1 Samuel 25:1b-42.

David has been on the run from the king for quite a while when this story happens. At the end of the story he'll be on the run for quite a while longer.

1. The name Nabal means "fool." How did this man show his foolishness?

2. What did Abigail do for David?

3. Why did she want to help him?

4. You may be in a situation where you want to show hospitality, but certain key family members don't. What can you learn from Abigail about dealing with a situation like that?

5. David was on the run from King Saul. It wasn't politically correct to help him. What "incorrect" people might God want you to show kindness to?

Read Proverbs 11:24-25.

1. There's an economic principle here. Can you state it in a way that would please an economics teacher?

2. Now can you state it in a way a six-year-old would get?

3. When you go to the movies, what refreshments do you buy? What do you like about these particular products?

4. Of all the people you saw yesterday, who most needed refreshing?

5. What could you have done or said to refresh them?

6. Now, how can you send out invitations (Action Step 3) to people you run into in the next couple of days?

The 3TC Chart

To, Through, and Talk About It!

Day 1   To _____

       Through _____

Day 2   To _____

       Through _____

Day 3   To _____

       Through _____

Day 4   To _____

       Through _____

Day 5   To _____

       Through _____

Day 6   To _____

       Through _____

       Talk About It _____

Day 7   To _____

       Through _____

Day 8   To _____

       Through _____

Day 9   To _____

       Through _____

Day 10   To _____

       Through _____

Day 11   To _____

       Through _____

Day 12   To _____

       Through _____

Day 13   To _____

       Through _____

       Talk About It _____

Day 14   To _____

       Through _____

Day 15   To _____

       Through _____

Day 16   To _____

       Through _____

Day 17   To _____

       Through _____

Day 18   To _____

       Through _____

Day 19   To _____

       Through _____

Day 20   To _____

       Through _____

       Talk About It _____

Day 21   To _____

       Through _____

Day 22   To _____

       Through _____

Day 23   To _____

       Through _____

Day 24   To _____

       Through _____

Day 25   To _____

       Through _____

Day 26   To _____

       Through _____

Each day write down how you've been part of the 24/7 church. What has God done TO you. What has God done THROUGH you. And each week record who you TALKED ABOUT IT with.

Day 27   To _____
         Through _____
         Talk About It _____

Day 28   To _____
         Through _____

Day 29   To _____
         Through _____

Day 30   To _____
         Through _____

Day 31   To _____
         Through _____

Day 32   To _____
         Through _____

Day 33   To _____
         Through _____

Day 34   To _____
         Through _____
         Talk About It _____

Day 35   To _____
         Through _____

Day 36   To _____
         Through _____

Day 37   To _____
         Through _____

Day 38   To _____
         Through _____

Day 39   To _____
         Through _____

Day 40   To _____
         Through _____

Day 41   To _____
         Through _____
         Talk About It _____

Day 42   To _____
         Through _____

Day 43   To _____
         Through _____

Day 44   To _____
         Through _____

Day 45   To _____
         Through _____

Day 46   To _____
         Through _____

Day 47   To _____
         Through _____

Day 48   To _____
         Through _____

Day 49   To _____
         Through _____

Day 50   To _____
         Through _____
         Talk About It _____

Friday Date

Read Hebrews 13:1-3.

When it comes to love, the New Testament gets very specific. There's a Greek word that describes perfect, unconditional, godly love no matter what. You probably know that word; it's agapé. There's a different word for erotic, sexual love and yet another one for the love shared by family members who really care for each other. The word for love in this passage has to do with good friends bound together because they have so much in common. If we picture lovers standing face to face, we would picture these friends side by side looking forward together.

1. How is "true Christian love" or "brotherly love" different from your everyday, ordinary love?

2. In today's society, we show hospitality to those we know. What opportunities do you have to show hospitality to those you don't know?

3. These Bible verses mention the possibility of entertaining angels without knowing it. Could that really happen?

4. Write up a brief plot line for "Touched By an Angel" based on these verses. Or try "The Simpsons."

Back Talk

"**D**ON'T YOU TALK back to me!"

We learned a long time ago that sassing the authorities didn't work. Talk back to a parent or teacher, and you'll wind up grounded or writing on the chalkboard.

Some of us learn to make wisecracks under our breath, loud enough so our friends laugh, but soft enough that we can blame someone else. But most people just give up. Sure, you may have a better idea, but no one wants to hear it. Go with the flow. Just don't talk back. That's not a good plan.

Major corporations know they need feedback. When Nike makes a new super-sneaker, they give a few hundred to basketball players and ask them, "What do you think? Did you jump higher, run faster, look cooler? Then they use the responses to improve the shoe. When they make a new shoe *commercial,* they pay people to sit and watch it. They need to know how people will respond! If someone says, "I don't get it," they reply, "Perfect! It's a Nike commercial. You're not supposed to."

Why should churches be any different? Don't pastors need feedback, too? Don't church school teachers and youth leaders need to know when they're scoring and when they've shot an airball? If the church will ever unleash its power, we will need to learn how to talk honestly about what we do there. Pastors have plenty of polite parishioners who file past them nodding and smiling (when, during the sermon, they were nodding and snoring). They need people who will lovingly tell them how they're doing. We could say the same for youth leaders and other teachers in the church. You probably have several people who minister to your spiritual needs. But have you ever told them *what* you need?

Be very careful about this, though. The Book of Proverbs tells us, "Some people make cutting remarks, but the words of the wise bring healing" (Proverbs 12:18). You want to speak with wisdom. There's a compact phrase in the New Testament that guides us through this process: "hold to the truth in love" (Ephesians 4:15). Try to keep truth and love in balance.

It's always easy to criticize. You can easily get into a rut of cynicism, where there is something wrong with everything, where whatever anyone says is boring or dumb or tacky or yesterday's guacamole. (And I admit, the guacamole reference is both dumb and tacky.) But truly helpful feedback comes from a humble heart.

"Be honest in your estimate of yourselves," the apostle Paul wrote, "measuring your value by how much faith God has given you" (Romans 12:3). I know this may come as a shock, but you don't know everything. *But* you are the all-time world-expert in one field: *what gets through to you.* You need to share your comprehensive knowledge of that field with the people who are trying to get through to you. Let them teach you, but use your constructive criticism to *help* them teach you.

The Bible talks about Christians having different gifts and doing different jobs in the church. We should be helping each other do those jobs. Your teachers need to help you grow in Christ and develop your gifts, and you should be helping them help you.

BaCkChECk BaCkChECk

Check the box if you have completed the assignment.

❑ I read chapter 3 in *When the Troops Are Tired.*

❑ I did Days 14–20.

❑ I prayed the "Good Grief" Prayer (p. 8).

❑ I took a 24/7 check on pages 40–41 (p. 9).

❑ I talked about my 24/7 experiences once this week to someone (Action Step 2, p. 9).

❑ I sent out invitations (p. 10).

❑ I read page 43 (Back Talk).

❑ I memorized a Bible verse this week (Bonus).

CominG AttRacTioNs

PowerPoint 4: Back Talk

Daily Assignments:

● Read the assigned Bible passages and answer the questions in the journal.

● Pray the "Good Grief" Prayer (p. 8).

● Take a 24/7 check on pages 40–41 (p. 9).

Assignments for this week:

● Read chapter 4 in *When the Troops Are Tired.*

● Talk about a 24/7 experience to someone at least once this week (p. 9).

● Bonus: Memorize the Bible verses that power you up.

Before the End:

● Send out invitations (p. 10).

● Give someone a piece of your mind (Action Step 4, p. 12).

Still to Come:

● Get hungry (Action Step 5, p. 13).

Back Talk

Read Exodus 17:8-13.

After God rescued his people from Egypt, he showed them over and over that he can be trusted—and that his style is, shall we say, distinctive.

1. To the best of your ability, draw a cartoon or picture of this scene.

2. What brand of deodorant did Moses use?

3. What role did Aaron and Hur play in this battle?

4. Obviously, Moses exerted some supernatural spiritual leadership in this battle. Who are your spiritual leaders?

5. What can you do to "hold up their arms" and help them "win the battle"?
   ❑ Pray for them
❑ Pay attention to them
   ❑ Encourage them
      ❑ Let them know what's going on in your life
         ❑ Speak highly of them to others

❑ Other? _____

Monday
Date

Read John 8:12-30.

1. Have you ever wished you could question something said during church or youth group? What do you think about Jesus allowing the Pharisees to challenge what he was saying?

2. If someone in your church or youth group has questions, what opportunities does he or she have to ask them?

3. If a non-Christian wanted to ask questions about your church's beliefs, what opportunities would there be?

4. If your pastor or youth leader came to you and asked how he or she could find out what kids your age need from church and youth group and what questions they have, what suggestions would you give?

5. Consider sharing your answer to question 4 as part of "giving someone a piece of your mind" for Action Step 4.

Read Nehemiah 8:1-12.

Seven months after the Israelites returned to their homeland from Babylon, they gathered in Jerusalem with one object in mind: to hear from God.

1. About how long did Ezra read from Scripture?

2. How did people respond?

3. What were the Levites doing?

4. Why do you think the people were weeping?

5. What do you usually do after hearing someone preach or teach from the Bible?
❑ Go back to sleep
　　　　　❑ Put the teaching into practice
　　　❑ Try to figure out what it means
　　　　　　　❑ Tell someone else about it
❑ Block it out of my mind
　　　　　❑ Study the text in the original Greek or Hebrew

6. Has the reading or preaching of the Bible ever had a great impact on you (as it did with Ezra's hearers)? When?

Read 2 Thessalonians 3:1-5.

1. What did Paul (the author) want the people to pray for?

2. Why did Paul want prayer for himself and other ministers?

3. How can you fill your day with God's Word?
❏ Never stop reading it
  ❏ Put biblical words on your T-shirt
    ❏ Put a New Testament in your back pocket
      ❏ Live out the Bible's teachings
  ❏ Talk with others about what the Bible says
    ❏ Spray scriptural graffiti on the walls of your home
❏ Other _____

4. Write a brief prayer here for your pastor or youth leader.

5. List the teachers, pastors, or leaders who have had the most spiritual impact on your life.

6. Consider telling the people you wrote down for question 5 the impact they've had on your life as part of "giving someone a piece of your mind" (Action Step 4).

uNanswered uNanswered?s

Read Matthew 7:24-29.

1. Write four to eight lines of a rap song or alternative lyric based on this story.

2. What is the "rock"?

3. How did the listeners respond after Jesus finished teaching?

4. How can the Word of God have more authority in your life?

5. Spiritually speaking, are the following (in your humble opinion) built on rock or sand?

	Rock	Sand
City hall	❑	❑
Your high school	❑	❑
Your church	❑	❑
Pizza Hut	❑	❑
Your youth group meeting place	❑	❑
Biggest bank in town	❑	❑
The local mall	❑	❑
Your home	❑	❑
Video store	❑	❑
Your coolest coffee shop	❑	❑

6. How can you help your teachers teach with "real authority"?

Friday Date

Read Acts 17:10-12, 16-34.

This passage falls in the middle of a nonstop, multi-city, gospel tour. Well, nonstop may not be accurate: they made frequent stops for lengthy conversations, riots, beatings, death plots, and nights in jail.

1. What were the Bereans like?

2. How did they respond to the preaching they heard?

3. Obviously, Paul spoke from the Hebrew Scriptures (what we call the Old Testament) while he was in Berea. But he didn't do this in Athens! Why not?

4. Paul regularly tied his message in with the culture of his hearers—what they read, what they thought, how they saw the world. What can you do to help your teachers understand your culture?

5. List five things from your culture—TV shows, movies, celebrities, magazines, music, slang, activities—that your pastor or youth leader (pick one) probably isn't familiar with.

POWErPoINt 5

Fast Times

LET'S SAY YOU'RE on a mission trip. Your youth group has traveled to a third-world country, an inner-city area, or a home in your community, and you have a job to do. Now, mission trips can be a lot of fun. And let's say you spend the first day or two getting more paint on your friends than on the walls.

At some point the leader has to say, "Come on, guys. There's nothing wrong with fun, but we came here to work—we need to get down to business." The Christian life is a lot like that. We need joy and celebration, but every so often we also need to buckle down and get busy. Sometimes we need to work at growing spiritually, committing ourselves to the Lord. There is plenty of time for feasting, but we also need time for fasting.

At first, fasting seems like a strange idea. "You mean go without food on *purpose?*" Then it sounds like dieting. "Oh, good, I'll be able to shed some unwanted poundage." But it's actually a practice that people of faith have done through the ages for *spiritual* purposes. Somehow, fasting can bring us closer to God.

How does this work? Well, it's a bit mysterious, but it's probably like this.

Food is very important to us. If we never eat, we'll die. Because of that, you could say it's the most basic need we have. Yet people need more than bread; they must feed on the Word of God (Matthew 4:4). Our relationship with God should be just as important to us as food, even more so. So, how do we show it? By going without food for a period of time and focusing on prayer. It's a way of showing God (and ourselves) that we mean business in our relationship with him.

In Scripture, fasting is usually linked with prayer. It's also connected with repentance. If you're sorry for sin, fasting is a way of showing that you're serious about coming back to God. The Bible also cautions us about fasting. First, *don't get the idea that food is bad.* Jesus often dined with people (Matthew 11:19), and even used a miracle to feed a crowd (John 6). All we're saying when we fast is that God is more important than even his great gift of food.

Second, *don't get proud about your fasting.* Without humility, you're missing the point—just like the Pharisee in Jesus' story, who boasted in prayer, "I fast twice a week, and I give you a tenth of my income." God preferred the prayer of the tax collector who pleaded, "O God, be merciful to me, for I am a sinner" (Luke 18:10–14).

Third, *don't get legalistic about it.* God isn't going to zap you if you break your 24-hour fast at the 23-hour mark. And don't make rules for other people. Decide with God what kind of fast to follow and use your God-given common sense in following it. Remember: the purpose is to develop your relationship with God (Luke 5:33–35).

Finally, while it can add power to our prayer life, *fasting is not an end in itself.* It must be accompanied by a commitment to stay close to God and to obey him. So don't let your fasting entirely end when you eat again. Let that brief, foodless time propel you into a more faithful life.

BaCkCheCk
BaCkCheCk

Check the box if you have completed the assignment.

❑ I read chapter 4 in *When the Troops Are Tired*.
❑ I did Days 21–27.
❑ I prayed the "Good Grief" Prayer.
❑ I took a 24/7 check on pages 40–41 (p. 9).
❑ I talked about my 24/7 experiences once this week to someone (p. 9).
❑ I sent out invitations (p. 10).
❑ I gave someone a piece of my mind (p. 12).
❑ I read page 51 (Fast Times).
❑ I memorized a Bible verse this week (Bonus).

Coming Attractions

PowerPoint 5: Fast Times

Daily Assignments:
● Read the assigned Bible passages and answer the questions in the journal.
● Pray the "Good Grief" Prayer (p. 8).
● Take a 24/7 check on pages 40–41 (p. 9).

Assignments for this week:
● Read chapter 5 in *When the Troops Are Tired*.
● Talk about a 24/7 experience to someone at least once this week (p. 9).
● Bonus: Memorize the Bible verses that power you up.

Before the End:
● Send out invitations (p. 10).
● Give someone a piece of your mind (p. 12).
● Get hungry (Action Step 5, p. 13).

Read Esther 4:12-17.

Esther became queen through a bizarre series of circumstances that put her in the right place at the right time to risk her life for God's people. Yikes!

1. This was clearly a crisis situation for Esther and Mordecai. How did they deal with it?

2. What good would it do to go without food in a situation like this?

3. What crisis situations has your family faced in the last year or two?

4. Would prayer and fasting have helped you deal differently with the crisis? If so, how?

5. Mordecai was convinced that God had a great purpose in putting Esther where she was (queen of Persia). Where has God placed you? What purposes might he have for you?

Read Matthew 4:1-11.

Jesus allowed John to baptize him at the Jordan River—actually, he insisted. Immediately after, the Father spoke his approval right out loud from heaven. Very impressive. Then, just when you'd think Jesus would get on with the work of saving the world, he disappeared into the desert for reasons no one understood at the time.

1. Why was it important for Jesus to fast before facing temptation? How did that prepare him?

2. Is it significant that Jesus spent 40 days fasting in the desert? Who else spent 40 somethings wandering in the wilderness? Any connection?

3. How can you gain spiritual strength through fasting?

4. What does verse 4 tell you about how important food is?

5. What temptations have you faced in the past week? List as many as you can think of (you may use code words).

6. How well prepared were you for these temptations? How could you prepare better?

Read Ezra 8:21-23.

At long last, the Israelites were released to return to their homeland after decades of exile. But the way home was long and dangerous.

1. If Ezra appeared today on a cable or satellite TV channel, what channel would it be, and why?

2. What was the purpose of the fast Ezra called for?

3. What besides fasting did Ezra's group do?

4. What were the exciting results of their prayer and fasting (read the rest of chapter 8)?

5. Is there an area of your life where you could use a little of God's protection? If yes, what is it? Try praying about that while you "get hungry" for Action Step 5.

Wednesday Date

Read Matthew 6:5-18.

1. From this passage, list some "Do's" and "Don'ts" of fasting.

Do	Don't

2. If your heavenly Father already knows what you need (verse 8), why pray?

3. Let's say someone comes up to you and says, "I'm really impressed by the way you're fasting. It's clear that you're a very spiritual person." How do you respond?

4. Scripture regularly puts fasting together with prayer. Why? How do you think fasting could enhance prayer?

5. Is it possible to fast for the wrong reasons? Explain.

Read 2 Chronicles 20:1-21.

In the decades following Solomon's death, the nation of Israel changed kings about as often as a fifth-grade boy changes underwear—not every day, but more often than you'd think. Just kidding. It was actually a very difficult time for the kingdom.

1. Here's another crisis, this time involving King Jehoshaphat. What did he do about it?

2. What does it mean to seek "the Lord for guidance" (verse 3)?

3. The king got the whole nation to fast together. Is there value in group fasting? If so, what?

4. Is getting a bunch of your friends together to fast for a particular reason something you would like to try for Action Step 5 or maybe sometime in the future? If so, how are you going to approach them about it?

5. Jehoshaphat was counting on God to help him defeat his enemies. What enemies are you facing—morally, spiritually, physically, socially? How might fasting help you deal with them?

6. Chris Carter asks you to write an "X-Files" episode based on this story. How does the scientist Scully explain the effect of fasting? How does the "believer" Mulder explain it?

Scully:

Mulder:

Friday Daily

Read Acts 13:1-3.

1. There are two times of fasting in this short passage. Can you find them? What was the result of each?

First:

Second:

2. Do you think fasting could help you hear God's direction for your life? If so, how?

3. How many people in this story were fasting? _____

4. How many were sent out as missionaries? _____

5. How can your fasting help *someone else* to understand what God wants for them?

6. Action Step 5 is Get Hungry. If you've already completed your fast, write down how it went and what it was like. Did anything special happen? (If you have not completed this action step yet, make sure that you answer this question at some point, and write it down here or somewhere else.)

POWErPoINt 6

Telling Secrets

RICKI, MONTEL, SALLY JESSY, and too many others have built careers on their ability to pull secrets out of talk-show guests. As a result, we know a lot more about people than we really want to know.

But here's something funny. Talk-show guests can unveil all sorts of odd perversities on national TV, and no one bats an eye. But if someone claims to be a Christian, the host gets flustered. "That's, uh, fine for you, but it's a private matter." Religion routinely gets swept under the rug.

And it's probably the same way with you. Chances are, you know lots of details about your best friends—*except what they really think about Jesus*. In fact, it's likely nowadays that most of your classmates have heard "Jesus" more as a curse word than as the name of a historical hero or a beloved Lord. It's just not cool to talk about him.

I'm not suggesting that you immediately start badgering your buddies to "get saved, or go to hell!" Some Christians have a knack for turning every conversation toward Jesus, but if you don't have it, it's silly to try. ("I see the soccer team scored a goal. Well, my goal in life is to serve Jesus.") You don't have to be an evangelist, but be a *witness* (Acts 1:8), telling the truth, the whole truth, about what God is doing in your life. Share the Christ who is in you. That, the Bible says, is the secret God is dying to tell the world: Christ lives in you (Colossians 1:27).

"Live wisely among those who are not Christians, and make the most of every opportunity" the apostle Paul counseled. "Let your conversation be gracious and effective so that you will have the right answer for everyone" (Colossians 4:5–6). No obnoxious buttonholing here. But people will have questions, and we can share the secret of success.

But we have a hard time talking about Jesus with our *Christian* friends, too, don't we? You'll gab about last week's "Buzzkill" prank or your locker mate's latest body piercing, but doesn't God deserve at least equal time with these other subjects of conversation?

If you have ever been madly *in love*—and I mean heart-pounding, nail-biting, gut-grabbing, knee-knocking in *love*—your best friends probably got sick and tired of hearing you talk about it. But you couldn't help yourself. Your new boyfriend or girlfriend was the most important person in your life, and you wanted to tell everybody.

So how much does Jesus mean to you? How is God treating you, teaching you, testing you? What joys has he brought to your life? What miracles are you praying for?

And why are you keeping all this a secret?

BackCheck BackCheck

Check the box if you have completed the assignment.

❑ I read chapter 5 in *When the Troops Are Tired.*
❑ I did Days 28–34.
❑ I prayed the "Good Grief" Prayer.
❑ I took a 24/7 check on pages 40–41 (p. 9).
❑ I talked about my 24/7 experiences once this week to someone (p. 9).
❑ I sent out invitations (p. 10).
❑ I gave someone a piece of my mind (p. 12).
❑ I got hungry (p. 13).
❑ I read page 59 (Telling Secrets).
❑ I memorized a Bible verse this week (Bonus).

PowerPoint 6: Telling Secrets

Daily Assignments:
● Read the assigned Bible passages and answer the questions in the journal.
● Pray the "Good Grief" Prayer (p. 8).
● Take a 24/7 check on pages 40–41 (p. 9).

Assignments for this week:
● Read chapter 6 in *When the Troops Are Tired.*
● Talk about a 24/7 experience to someone at least once this week (p. 9).
● Bonus: Memorize the Bible verses that power you up.

Before the End:
● Send out invitations (p. 10).
● Give someone a piece of your mind (p. 12).
● Get hungry (p. 13).

Read Joshua 1:1-9.

Joshua was Moses' right-hand man. Now Moses was gone and, like it or not, Joshua was *the* man.

1. If you were to sum up this passage in a screen saver message for your computer, what would it be?

2. What reasons are given for Joshua to "be strong and courageous" (verse 6)?

3. How was Joshua supposed to treat the "Book of the Law" (verse 8)?

4. How can you treat the Bible that way?
❑ Read it regularly
　　　　❑ Think about it during TV commercials
　　　❑ Get key Bible verses tattooed on strategic body parts
❑ Make sure every homework assignment quotes at least one Bible text
　　　　❑ Hold up a "John 3:16" sign at football games
❑ Offer your friends encouragement based on the Bible
　　　　❑ Get involved in a small group Bible study
　　　❑ Put Bible readings on a cassette and listen as you drive
　　　　　　❑ Memorize your favorite Bible verses
　　　❑ Scrawl 2 Thessalonians 3:10 on your refrigerator
❑ Put a loudspeaker on your car and drive around preaching
　　　　❑ Create a "Bible virus" and infect offensive Web sites

Monday Date

Read Psalm 105:1-45.

After David defeated his archenemies, the Philistines, and made Israel safe for theocracy, he built a place in Jerusalem for the Ark of the Covenant—the special mobile container for the Ten Commandments and other symbols of God's relationship to his people. This is the psalm David prepared for the dedication ceremony (1 Chronicles 14–16).

1. What are the five most impressive things God did for his people, as described in this passage?

2. If you were to write a similar psalm about your life, what five things would you talk about that God has done for you?

3. If you put your psalm to music, what kind of song would it be, and why?

4. From the first five verses of Psalm 105, list five things we are asked to do.

5. How and when will you do one of these things today or tomorrow?

Read John 9:11-41.

1. What had happened to the blind man?

2. What sort of reaction did he get to his story?

3. What support did he get from his parents?

4. Notice that the leaders kept dragging the man into theological discussion. They insulted him. They thought he was preaching to them when he was really just answering their questions. What is the "one thing" the man did know (verse 25 NIV)?

5. If you could boil your testimony about Jesus down to "one thing," what would it be?

6. How do you think others have misunderstood you when you've told your "secrets"?

Read Acts 26:1-32.

Paul was no stranger to danger. At a particularly dicey moment, Paul used his Roman citizenship to get his case transferred from the Jewish courts, where they plotted to kill him, to the Roman legal system and the court of last appeal, the emperor himself. King Agrippa agreed to hear Paul's case in order to clarify the charges against him before sending him on to Rome.

1. Why was it important for Paul to tell the "secret" of his life before he met Jesus?

2. If you were to make Paul's story into a major motion picture, what kind of special effects would you use?

3. Why did Governor Festus think Paul was insane?

4. If you could pick some famous person to tell about Jesus, who would it be?

5. Let's say you had five minutes with that person to "tell your secret." What would you say?

6. Do you think it's possible to make someone a Christian so quickly (verse 28)?

Read Leviticus 23:33-43.

At first glance this looks like the rest of Leviticus—a bunch of boring rules to follow. But *see* what it's describing: a party.

1. How many times is the word *celebrate* mentioned?

2. What was the purpose of this celebration?

3. What celebrations could you have in your life (or in your youth group) to honor God for what he has done?

4. Note that this feast was to be an annual event. People would remember God's past actions by celebrating every year. What annual events are already part of your life?
❑ Super Bowl Sunday
❑ Last day of school
❑ April Fools' Day

List five others that you enjoy.
1.
2.
3.
4.
5.

5. What annual celebration could you begin—personally, in your family, in your youth group, or in your church—to commemorate God's past actions?

Friday Date

Read Judges 5:1-12.

When Moses died, Joshua led Israel. When Joshua died, things pretty much fell apart. The people hated the discipline of following God and got into serious trouble—like slavery for 8 years, 18 years, and 20 years (to name three occasions). Each time the people came to their senses, confessed their sins, and asked for God's help, he gave them a judge to deliver them from their oppressors. Deborah was one of those judges. Barak was the soldier she enlisted to lead the troops.

1. Who was singing this song, and why?

2. Why do you think so many people in the Bible broke out into song when they started talking about God's actions?

3. What were the musicians (verse 11) doing at the watering holes?

4. Is there some event of the past six months or so that convinced you that God was actively working in your life? (If not, go back a year or two.) What happened?

5. How many people have you told about this God-event?

6. What do you think would happen if you told more people this "telling secret"?

POWErPOINt 7

Cross Purposes

I (RANDY) THOUGHT I was the only Christian in my high school. My church had a great youth group, but it was in another town and all the kids went to other schools.

Some of my school friends went to church with their families, but I was suspicious of the denominations of those churches. Were they "real" Christians or just churchgoers? Since my friends didn't talk much about their faith, I assumed they weren't real Christians.

Now I look back and wonder how many of those friends were a lot like me, lonely in their faith, lacking support, trusting Christ but tossed around by temptation. If I had only looked past the church labels and made a connection, we could have helped each other.

In my senior year, I finally found a few other Christians and we started an after-school Bible study. I was expecting three, maybe five, to show up. We had about fifteen. People I had been sitting with, eating with, walking the halls with for four years of high school, were telling me that they were Bible-believing Christians. It was great to learn this, but I was sorry we hadn't connected earlier.

There is power in numbers. But, more than that, there is power in *connections*. I strengthen you and you strengthen me—*if* we agree that we worship the same Lord. As lonely individuals, we will shrink from the challenges that face us. But when we connect with others, we gain confidence.

You may have wondered why there are so many different denominations of Christian churches. The divisions exist for many reasons—historical, political, and doctrinal—and they're probably impossible to undo. *But we can reach across the lines.* Baptists and Bible churches, Presbyterians and Pentecostals, conservatives and liberals, all of us can come together to celebrate our common love of the Lord. In Bible studies at work or in school, in community worship times, in public prayer meetings, we can focus on unity rather than division.

Jesus prayed for the unity of his followers (John 17:21–23), and Paul wrote about it: "There is only one Lord, one faith, one baptism, and there is only one God and Father, who is over us all and in us all and living through us all" (Ephesians 4:5–6). But too often we are at cross-purposes, when we should be at Cross purposes. If Shaq and Kobe Bryant grab a rebound at the same time, do they fight over it? "Same team!" they'd say. And we should have that same understanding among different churches. Same team! Rather than pursuing our own church agendas, we should be seeking to work together to honor Christ.

We will always disagree on some points. And you will encounter "Christian" kids who wear strange T-shirts or tattoos, who use language you find offensive, who engage in activities you disapprove of. You don't have to approve of everything they believe or do. But if they will join with you in praising the crucified Christ and seeking his guidance, you have a teammate.

67

BaCkCheCk
BaCkCheCk

Check the box if you have completed the assignment.

❏ I read chapter 6 in *When the Troops Are Tired*.
❏ I did Days 35–41.
❏ I prayed the "Good Grief" Prayer.
❏ I took a 24/7 check on pages 40–41 (p. 9).
❏ I talked about my 24/7 experiences once this week to someone (p. 9).
❏ I sent out invitations (p. 10).
❏ I gave someone a piece of my mind (p. 12).
❏ I got hungry (p. 13).
❏ I read page 67 (Cross Purposes).
❏ I memorized a Bible verse this week (Bonus).

CoMiNg AttRacTioNs

PowerPoint 7: Cross Purposes
PowerPoint 8: Power Up

Daily Assignments:
● Read the assigned Bible passages and answer the questions in the journal.
● Pray the "Good Grief" Prayer (p. 8).
● Take a 24/7 check on pages 40–41 (p. 9).

Assignments for this week:
● Read chapters 7 and 8 in *When the Troops Are Tired*.
● Read page 74 (Power Up).
● Talk about a 24/7 experience to someone at least once this week (p. 9).
● Bonus: Memorize the Bible verses that power you up.

Before the End:
● Send out invitations (p. 10).
● Give someone a piece of your mind (p. 12).
● Get hungry (p. 13).

Read 3 John: 1-14.

John's second letter warns against accepting outsiders who come teaching something other than the Gospel of Jesus Christ. His third letter warns against rejecting those who come teaching the truth.

1. Who was writing to whom?

2. What do we learn about Gaius from the letter itself?

3. "The friends" ("brothers", NIV) in verse 5 were traveling preachers. What was Gaius doing for them? What was Diotrephes doing?

4. How do you react to people in your school or community from different denominations?
❏ Who cares about denominations?
       ❏ They're not *real* Christians
   ❏ Scum of the earth
❏ They're all right, as long as they wear name tags with the name of their church
      ❏ OK, but don't trust them
   ❏ Fellow Christians! Praise God!
❏ They're probably trying to convert me
    ❏ Other _____

5. How do you know when someone else is a "true" Christian?

Read 2 Chronicles 10:12-11:14

After Solomon died, his son Rehoboam took the throne and generally made a mess of everything.

1. Jeroboam was leading a rebellion because King Rehoboam was treating the people harshly. The elders had advised the king to loosen up, but what did King Rehoboam do instead?

2. What was God's message to the king in 2 Chronicles 11:4?

3. Why would someone continue a course of division and battling even when God clearly has a different idea?

The civil war between Rehoboam and Jeroboam tore the nation of Israel apart and hurt both sides. Rehoboam's father was the mighty King Solomon, whose wealth and power were world-renowned, but never again would ancient Israel be a major power in the Mideast.

4. Divisions like this have plagued the church for centuries. Most of the different denominations we now have are the results of rebellions against other denominations. (Some of these rebellions, like Jeroboam's, had good causes, but the fighting has created a lot of bad blood and ill will.) Chances are, you won't be able to put denominations back together, but you may be able to connect with a Christian of another church. How will you do this?

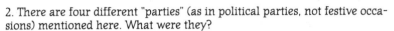

Read 1 Corinthians 1:10-17.

1. Name a team you root for that benefits from teamwork.

2. There are four different "parties" (as in political parties, not festive occasions) mentioned here. What were they?

   1.

   2.

   3.

   4.

3. Why was Paul glad that he had only personally baptized a few people there?

4. Have you ever seen people get so jazzed about a particular leader that they seem to forget about Christ? If so, when? Who? What could you do about it?

5. When Christians have divisions between them, what's usually the problem?

6. What can we do to ensure that we "stop arguing" or "agree with one another" (NIV) and start finding "cross purposes"?

Read Psalm 133:1-3.

1. You've been asked to design a greeting card with verse 1 on the inside. What's on the cover?

2. What's the best time of Christian unity you have ever experienced? With a friend? With a church group of some kind? Tell about it.

3. What's the best thing about getting along with other Christians? What's "pleasant" about it?

4. What can you do this week to promote the cause of unity and "cross purposes"?

Read John 17:6-26.

Just hours—maybe just minutes—before he was arrested, while his disciples listened, Jesus prayed for them. Imagine Jesus praying for you in these words.

1. In verse 20, Jesus prays for "all who will ever believe . . . because of [the disciples'] testimony." Like who? Name one.

2. In three words or less, sum up the theme of this passage.

3. What does it mean to "be one"?

4. How can the church's unity mirror the unity of Jesus with the Father?

5. According to verse 23, what is the result of the church's unity?

POWErPOINt 8

Power Up

A MAN RUSHES OUT to CompUSA to buy the latest greatest computer he can find, dripping with memory and megahertz. It even plays games *for* you.

The man hurries home and sets it up, carefully connecting all the cables. He can't wait to use this awesome machine. But he has one question: How do you turn it on? I think we'd all be surprised how many calls to the techs are exactly that—*How do I power up?*

But isn't that the question we're all asking *in life*? We sleepwalk through our days, doing the same-old same-old, hoping for a jumpstart of some kind. How can we realize our potential? How can we really make a difference?

As Christians, we have an amazing promise. "You will receive power" (Acts 1:8). God showed his stupendous power by raising Jesus from the dead (Romans 1:4), and he raises us, too, from our death-like existence (1 Corinthians 6:14).

Paul prayed that Christians would experience "the incredible greatness of [God's] power" (Ephesians 1:19). Later, he reminded his readers that God is "able to accomplish infinitely more than we would ever dare to ask or hope" (Ephesians 3:20).

"The Spirit of God, who raised Jesus from the dead, lives in you. And just as he raised Christ from the dead, he will give life to your mortal body by this same Spirit living within you" (Romans 8:11).

Is that enough megahertz for you? You've got the machine sitting there in front of you. Now, how do you power up?

Well, that's what this whole Adventure has been about, but let's take one more crack at some practices you can continue in the weeks and months ahead.

1. Pray without sneezing (1 Thessalonians 5:17). No, I'm sorry, the word is *ceasing*. Never stop! Of course, you'll need to open your eyes sometimes, but keep the communication open. It's like having a straight connection to the Net in your bedroom. You're always on.

2. Let go of your own power. If you try to dazzle folks with your own holiness, wisdom, or personal power—GAME OVER. The apostle Paul talked about himself and his fellow missionaries as "jars of clay" (NIV) holding the tremendous treasure of God's message. The purpose was "so everyone can see that our glorious power is from God and is not our own" (2 Corinthians 4:7). God once reminded a Jewish leader about his success: "It is not by force nor by strength, but by my Spirit" (Zechariah 4:6).

3. Let God use your weakness. What are you not so good at? That may be the way God will use you. Don't ask me how or why, but God said, "My power works best in your weakness" (2 Corinthians 12:9).

4. Take a chance. Sometimes you just have to step forward and trust that God's power will be there when you need it. "For God has not given us a spirit of fear and timidity, but of power, love, and self-discipline" (2 Timothy 1:7).

God's power is available for us to use. Jesus' resurrection was a phenomenal test-drive. Now it's time for you to get behind the wheel.

Friday Date

Read Romans 8:28-39.

Paul writes the Christians in Rome to help them understand the vast difference between the righteousness that comes from self–discipline and the righteousness that comes by faith in Jesus. The first passes through pride on the way to failure and death. The second passes through humility on the way to a glorious future with God.

1. What's the answer to verse 31?

2. What's the answer to verse 32?

3. If you made a multiple-choice test out of this passage, what would it look like?

4. Based on this passage, where can you find power for your life?

5. How will these verses help you find power in the next few days?

Read Philippians 3:7-11.

1. If Paul was an accountant, what would he put on the profit side of his balance sheet, and what's on the loss side?

Profit | **Loss**

2. If there ever was a chance to put a naughty word in Scripture, it's here in verse 8. In the original Greek, the word for garbage is not something you'd use in polite company. Why do you think Paul used such a strong word?

3. What did Paul want to know and experience about Christ?

4. Paul had a religious past, but he decided not to put any trust in that. Instead, he'd be fully devoted to Christ. What have you been putting your trust in?

5. In the next month, how can you go *all out* for Jesus? What would that look like?

Read 1 Corinthians 15:1-11.

1. According to this text, what are the basics of the gospel?

2. In verses 9–11, what's the secret of Paul's success?

3. In 23 words or less, what do you believe about the resurrection of Jesus Christ?

4. How does the resurrection of Jesus affect your daily life?

5. When this Adventure is over, how will you continue to tap into God's power each day? What's your ongoing plan?

BaCkCheCk
BaCkCheCk

Check the box if you have completed the assignment.

- ❏ I read chapters 1–8 in *When the Troops Are Tired.*
- ❏ I did Days 1–50.
- ❏ I prayed the "Good Grief" Prayer.
- ❏ I took 24/7 checks on pages 40–41.
- ❏ I talked about my 24/7 experiences once a week to someone.
- ❏ I sent out invitations.
- ❏ I gave someone a piece of my mind.
- ❏ I got hungry.
- ❏ I memorized Bible verses.

Coming AttRacTioNs

By now I'm sure you're ready to just keep going. Well, if you don't want to stop all the good things—like daily Bible study and prayer—that you've been doing these last 50 days, we have a couple of suggestions for you.

1. Other Adventures
Why not try it again. There are a lot of other 50-Day Adventures for you to get going on. We've suggested a couple on the inside back cover of this journal. Use the order form on page 80 or give us a call at 1-800-224-2735, and we'll suggest the Adventure that is perfect for you.

2. One to One & Discovery
Scripture Union Devotionals
Scripture Union subscriptions are for a whole year! There are devotionals for all ages. *One to One* is for ages 11–14 and *Discovery* is a personal application guide for mature young people and adults. These devotionals will get you into God's word and help you continue the disciplines you've started during this Adventure. Check out the order form on page 80 for everything you need to know.

last words

TELL US YOUR STORY

We've been praying that this Adventure would make a difference in your life. And we would love to hear your story. As you're finishing up this Adventure, we're already hard at work on a new one. But the Adventure is for you. So send us your comments and feedback. We'd love to hear from you.

Mainstay Church Resources
Editorial Department
PO Box 30
Wheaton, IL 60189

Or send an e-mail with your comments to: T50DSA@aol.com

SO, YOU'VE FINISHED THE ADVENTURE!

Daily Bible reading and prayer have been a part of your life for the past 50 days. But while the Adventure ends after 50 days, the habits you formed don't need to. Consider these other Adventures to keep you going on the path you've started on.

• The In the House 50-Day Spiritual Adventure

In the House Student Journal	$6.00
I Like Church, But . . . Guidebook	$6.00

• The I'm So Confused 50-Day Spiritual Adventure

I'm So Confused! Student Journal	$6.00
When Life Becomes a Maze Guidebook	$6.00

For info on additional 50-Day Spiritual Adventures write, call, or e-mail Mainstay Church Resources.

ORDER FORM

	Price	Qty	Total
Student's Life Application Bible, New Living Translation	$20.00	_____	_____
In the House 50-Day Spiritual Adventure			
In the House Student Journal	$6.00	_____	_____
*I Like Church, But...*Guidebook	$6.00	_____	_____
I'm So Confused 50-Day Spiritual Adventure			
I'm So Confused Student Journal	$6.00	_____	_____
*When Life Becomes a Maze But...*Guidebook	$6.00	_____	_____
		Subtotal	_____
Add 10% for UPS shipping/handling ($4.00 minimum)			_____
Canadian or Illinois residents add 7% GST/sales tax			_____
		TOTAL	_____

Scripture Union Guides

All devotionals will be sent every three months for one year (tax and shipping included).
Yes! I would like an annual subscription to:

	Price	Qty	Total
Discovery	$20.00	_____	_____
One to One	$20.00	_____	_____
		TOTAL	_____

TOTAL AMOUNT ENCLOSED _____

Please fill out the information below:

Your name _____

Address _____

State/Prov _____Zip/Code _____Phone _____

I'd like to pay by: ☐ Check ☐ Money Order ☐ VISA ☐ MasterCard ☐ Discover

Send this form with your check to Mainstay Church Resources, Box 30 Wheaton, IL 60189. In Canada: The Chapel Ministries, Box 2000, Waterdown, ON LOR 2HO. Or call 1-800-224-2735 (in Canada 1-800-461-4114) for credit card orders.

MO7SJ98